# A B C

# Farm Animals Book

AO PRESS

## Jessica Lee Anderson

To Lacey Proffitt—thanks for all you do for many different kinds of farm animals and for sharing your agricultural knowledge with us! - JLA

Photo credits—Front Cover: Grigory Bruev, Elena Photo, Ken Wiedemann, Life On White; Back Cover: Life On White (all); Cover Page: Grigory Bruev, Elena Photo, Ken Wiedemann, Nynke van Holten (sheep and ducklings), Life On White (pig), Copyright page: Life On White, Billion Photos; Dedication page: Nynke van Holten; p. 4: GoldCoinz, Mehgan Murphy; p. 5: Lakeview_Images; p. 6: PahaM; p. 7: Life On White; p.8: Nigelb10; p. 9: Life On White; p. 10: JZHunt; p. 11: emholk; p. 12: shellhawker; p. 13: Auldist; p. 14: cordimages; p. 15: Life On White, p. 16: Travelarium; p. 17: starfish123; p. 18: cynoclub; p. 19: Nynke van Holten, p. 20: Kerrick; p. 21: Los Muertos Crew; p. 22: Life On White; p. 23: claudiovizia; p. 24: Stephane Bidouze; p. 25: Fernando Cortes; p. 26: Frank Manzo; p. 27: Julia Chan; p. 28: MikeLane45; p. 29: ugurhan; p. 30: Life On White (Highland Cattle and Angora Goat); p. 31: Michael Anderson

# This Book Belongs to:

_____

#  is for Alpacas

Alpacas are small, gentle relatives of camels. There are two types of alpacas—<u>huacayas</u> with teddy-bear-like fleece and <u>suris</u> with dreadlock-like fleece.

# B is for Bobwhite Quail

Bobwhite Quail get their name from their whistling call that sounds like "bobwhite." Quail are kept on different kinds of farms, and they live on the ground.

# C is for Crested Ducks

**Crested Ducks have a funny hairdo with a little ball of feathers on the top of their heads. Female ducks are called hens or ducks while male ducks are called drakes, and their babies are called ducklings.**

# D is for Donkeys

Donkeys can be found throughout the world, and they are known for being smart, calm, and hardworking. There are different types of breeds that range in size from Miniature Donkeys to large American Mammoth Jackstock Donkeys.

# E is Exmoor Ponies

The Exmoor Pony is a type of small horse from Britain (where some still roam freely about). The Exmoor Pony can be fun for children to ride, and like other ponies, it is strong and can work hard.

# F is for French Lops

The French Lop is a large type of rabbit that can be friendly and cuddly. Rabbits get the zoomies like dogs, and they also can get the binkies—happy jumps with twists in the air!

#  is for Great Pyrenees

The Great Pyrenees is a type of large, powerful dog with a thick coat of fur. Like sheepdogs and shepherd dog breeds, this type of dog watches over animals on the farm such as sheep.

# is for Hereford Cattle

Hereford Cattle range from dark red to yellowish red, and they can live for many years. Grown female cattle are called cows, and grown males are called bulls—a baby is called a calf.

 is for ISA Brown Chickens

ISA Brown Chickens get along with people well, and the females (hens) lay many eggs. A male chicken is called a rooster, and baby chickens are called chicks.

# J is for Jersey Cattle

Jersey Cattle have large eyes, and they are popular on farms all over as the cows produce a lot of milk! Their milk is more nutritious compared to other types, and it is used to make things like cheese and butter.

# K is for Kunekune Pigs

Kunekune Pigs are originally from New Zealand, and they are a small, hairy pig that can graze on grass. Adult female pigs are called sows, adult male pigs are called boars, and baby pigs are called piglets.

# L is for Llamas

Llamas are related to camels just like alpacas, though llamas are larger, taller, and less shy than alpacas (they prefer to be alone rather than in a herd). A baby llama is called a cria.

#  is for Maine Coon Cats

Many cats live on farms including the Maine Coon, a type of cat with a fluffy tail, thick fur, and tufts of hair on the tips of their ears. Maine Coons are one of the largest cat breeds in the world!

#  is for Nigerian Dwarf Goats

Nigerian Dwarf Goats are a small goat breed originally from Africa, and the females (called does) make a good amount of milk. A grown-up male goat is called a buck or a billy goat, and baby goats are called kids.

#  is for Orpington Chickens

Orpington Chickens can come in colors like white, black, buff, and splash (which means white or grey with "splashes" of black or blue). Chickens make many sounds to communicate—even when chicks are inside the eggs!

# P is for Pygmy Goats

Pygmy Goats are gentle, friendly goats with short legs and round bodies. Goats make funny sounds (including screams), and they like to climb and explore.

# Q is for Quarter Horses

The Quarter Horse is a fast horse—the name comes from the horse's speed, running faster than other horse breeds in races of a quarter mile or less. A grown female horse is called a mare, a male is called a stallion, and a baby is called a foal.

# is for Royal Palm Turkeys

Royal Palm Turkeys have interesting feather colors, and like other turkeys, male turkeys called toms make "gobble-gobble" sounds. The flap over a turkey's beak is called a snood, and the skin around its neck is called a wattle.

# S is for Suffolk Sheep

**Suffolk Sheep are a popular type of sheep with black faces, and they don't have horns. Female sheep are called ewes, males are called rams, and baby sheep are called lambs.**

# is for Toulouse Geese

Toulouse Geese are large gray and white water-loving birds. A female goose is called a goose, a male is called a gander, and a baby is called a gosling.

#  is for Ushant Sheep

Ushant Sheep are also known as Ouessant Sheep, and they are one of the smallest breeds of sheep. Their thick fleece can be brown, white, or black, and it can be used for things like knitting yarn.

# V is for Vietnamese Pot-bellied Pigs

Vietnamese Potbelly Pigs are social, friendly pigs originally from Vietnam. They have wrinkled faces and bellies that hang low, nearly dragging to the ground.

# W is for Wiltshire Horn Sheep

Wiltshire Horn Sheep are active with long legs, and both males and females have horns. This breed of sheep has a type of wool that sheds naturally, meaning it doesn't need to be sheared like other types of sheep.

# is for Xinjiang Goats

![Xinjiang goats standing on a path near a red and white fence with grass in the background]

Xinjiang Goats are a type of goat originally from the mountains of Xinjiang in China. These goats have a type of soft, downy undercoat called cashmere that is used to make clothing.

# Y is for Yokohama Chickens

Yokohama Chickens have really long tail-feathers. They are small-sized chickens that are friendly and not as noisy as some other breeds of chickens.

# Z is for Zebu Cattle

**Zebu Cattle are sometimes called Camel Cows. They have large bones between their shoulders and a hump there that is made up of muscle and fat.**

# 5 Farm Animal Facts:

**1** Most sheep breeds have wool that keeps on growing and needs to be sheared so the animals stay cool and comfortable.

**2** Pigs roll around in the mud to stay cool, and the mud acts like a form of sunscreen.

**3** Horses don't sleep as much as some animals (such as cats). They can sleep standing up!

**4** Cattle and other grazing animals like sheep and goats have a dental pad instead of sharp upper teeth—allowing them to gather up grass and plants.

**5** Chickens are omnivores! In addition to plants and seeds, chickens sometimes eat insects or small animals.

Jessica Lee Anderson is an award-winning author of over 50 books for young readers. Jessica lives near Austin, Texas with her daughter, Ava, and husband, Michael. They are volunteer farm animal feeders at a living history museum called Pioneer Farms. You can learn more about Jessica by visiting www.jessicaleeanderson.com.

## Check out these other titles:

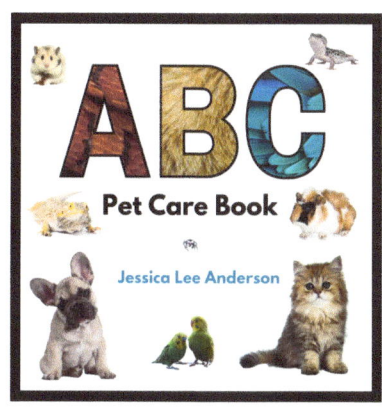

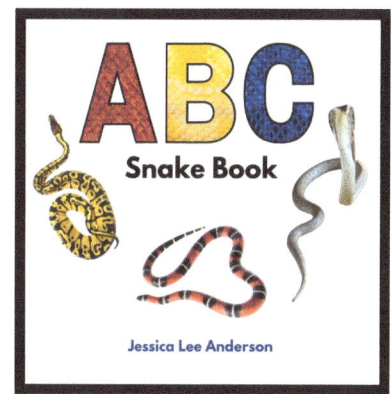